The WARLORD'S FISH

The WARLORD'S FISH

Virginia Walton Pilegard

Illustrated by
Nicolas Debon

PELICAN PUBLISHING COMPANY
Gretna 2002

To Will, Tim, Sarah, Mike, Maddie, and Anne,
whose internal compass led her from the
Middle Kingdom to my heart—VWP
To Vincent, Sylvie, Titouan, Prune, and Achim—ND

The word "Pelican" and the depiction of a pelican
are trademarks of Pelican Publishing Company, Inc.,
and are registered in the U.S. Patent and Trademark Office.

Library of Congress Cataloging-in-Publication Data

Pilegard, Virginia Walton.
   The Warlord's fish / Virginia Walton Pilegard ; illustrated by Nicolas Debon.
     p. cm.
  Summary: In ancient China, an artist and his young apprentice are kidnapped and taken
into the desert, where their captors' caravan is lost until the artist's carved wooden
goldfish points the way to safety.
   ISBN 1-56554-964-3
   [1. Compass—Fiction. 2. Artists—Fiction. 3. Voyages and travel—Fiction. 4. China—
History—To 221 B.C.—Fiction.] I. Debon, Nicolas, ill. II. Title.
   PZ7.P6283 Waq2002
   [Fic]—dc21
                                      2002001455

Printed in Korea

Published by Pelican Publishing Company, Inc.
1000 Burmaster Street, Gretna, Louisiana 70053

The Warlord's Fish

Glistening water filled the wide, blue bowl. A carved wooden fish floated in a gentle arc until its face pointed south to the river. Chuan, a young peasant boy who had become the apprentice of the most respected artist in China, reached to splash the water in the bowl. "You will teach me to make this, master?" he asked.

The artist nodded.

The boy dipped his hand once more and caught the small carving.

Suddenly he heard shouting in the courtyard, the raucous sounds of camels and foreigners. The warlord's palace, where he and the artist lived, must be receiving visitors.

"What are they saying?" the artist whispered.

Chuan knew some foreign words from his excursions to the market for the artist's supplies. "They say they have been cheated," he answered.

"Tell them the warlord is away," said the artist, pushing the boy ahead of him in the cold sunshine of the fall morning.

"We brought the finest jewels and spices!" snarled a bearded man who mixed Chinese words with his foreign tongue. "Yet this is all the silk your dishonest merchants give." He gestured at the packs tied to five camels. "Now, the thieves have closed their booth and left the market! I have been robbed."

"Tell them fine silk is most costly," said the artist.

The boy translated, adding, "In all the world, the Middle Kingdom is the only place a shrewd traveler such as yourself can buy such magnificent fabric."

"Who are you, boy?" the bearded trader growled. "Are you so smart you speak for the entire empire?"

"Only a humble apprentice," Chuan answered. "The lord of this palace is away, and my master and I have no way to help you until he returns."

The trader's teeth gleamed white in his dark beard. "A smart boy like you will bring almost as much as a scrap of your glowing silk." His hand closed over the back of Chuan's neck. "Take the artist too," another trader shouted. "He can pick up sticks for the fire and carry water, even if he won't bring much of a price."

Chuan and his teacher were bound and thrown onto the saddle of a complaining camel.

f or days they traveled along a well-marked road, which the artist said led to unknown lands beyond the civilized world. They secretly hoped to meet the returning warlord, riding his proud stallion, but instead they saw fewer and fewer travelers.

At last, they found themselves at the edge of a vast desert. The trader unpacked cloaks to cover their faces against the blowing sand.

That night, the air grew cold. Fierce winds tore at the tents he and his men tried to put up. Chuan and his master slept curled up against their disagreeable camel while the sand whispered sad, scary songs.

By morning, sand and pebbles covered the place where the trail had been. The trader pointed to the rising sun with his right arm. "East," he grunted, climbing onto his camel. "Straight ahead is north."

The weary caravan followed him across the trackless sand.

Chuan noticed a storm of blowing sand racing toward them. The sky turned dark and hid the late autumn sun. The caravan stopped. Everyone slid to the ground, covered their heads, and cowered against their kneeling camels.

When the wind died down, Chuan and the artist ate bits of the foreigners' spicy dried meat and drank sparingly from leather water bags. Clouds hid the stars and the singing sand became like the hooves of a hundred warlords' horses.

The next day, angry shouts awakened Chuan.

"You and your greedy haggling," one man bellowed. "We wasted too much time. Winter is upon us."

"We are lost," cried a second. "We will add our bones to the many who have died in this desert."

"Cowards! Go tend to your camels." The bearded trader's voice roared above the rest.

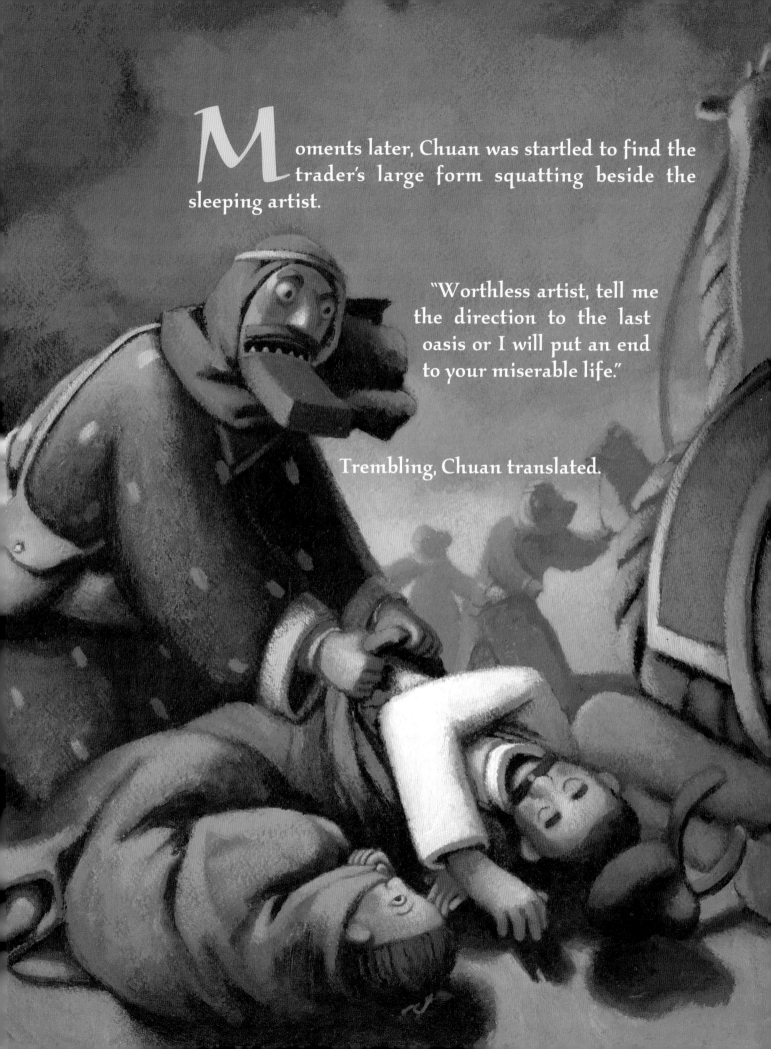

Moments later, Chuan was startled to find the trader's large form squatting beside the sleeping artist.

"Worthless artist, tell me the direction to the last oasis or I will put an end to your miserable life."

Trembling, Chuan translated.

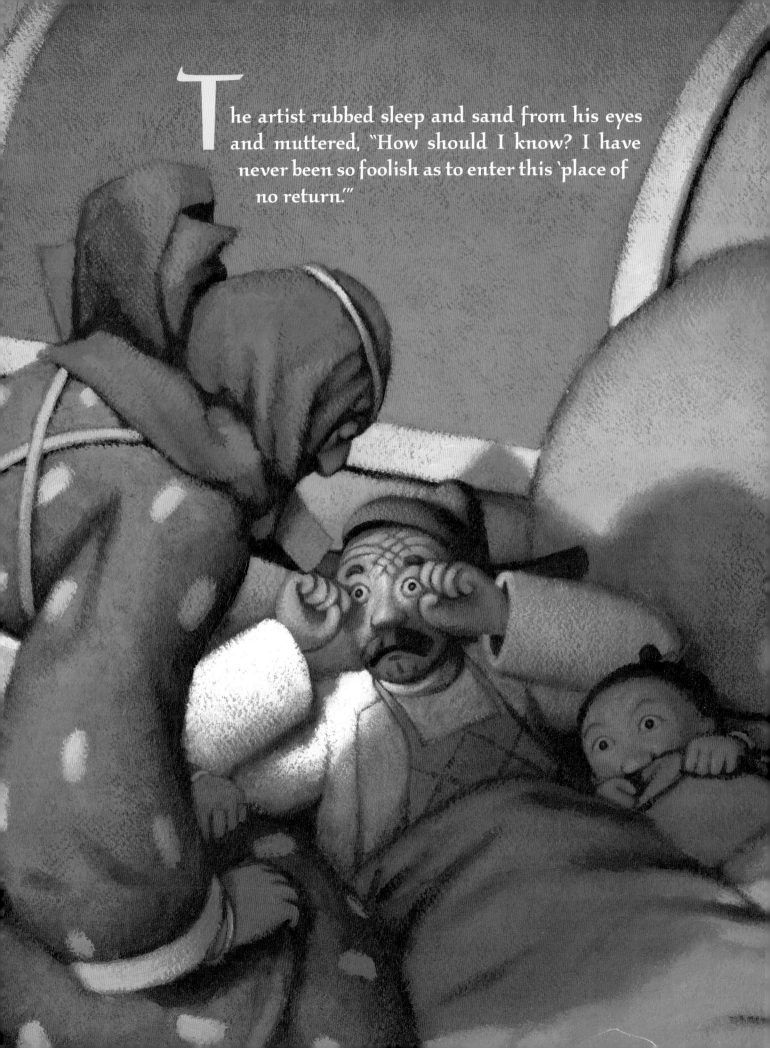

The artist rubbed sleep and sand from his eyes and muttered, "How should I know? I have never been so foolish as to enter this 'place of no return.'"

C huan hunched his shoulders and pushed his hands into his belt. His fingers brushed against a familiar wooden shape, the little fish that the artist had crafted. Gathering his courage he spoke boldly. "If you will give my master a bowl of water, he will tell you."

The trader's eyes grew as dark as the sky. "A bowl of our water? Would you dare to trick me?"

When they heard the word "water" the other men crowded around, arguing again.

"You will get us both killed," hissed the artist behind his hand.

"You said when this fish floats, its face always points south," Chuan whispered, giving the artist a glimpse of the wooden fish.

The bearded trader silenced everyone by lifting his own precious water bag. He poured every drop of his life-giving supply into a shallow bowl that someone fetched from the packs.

Chuan dropped the fish into the water as he had done so many days before.

A gust of wind whipped the bowl from the bearded trader's hands, spilling the contents on the desert sand. He scooped the little carving into his fist. "You thought this pitiful amulet would save you?"

"No, no," Chuan said. "There is a special stone set inside the fish, which makes it float in line with the pull of the earth. It always faces south."

"Tell him I saw which way the fish turned," the artist said.

"Our only hope is to trust the strange fish," the traders agreed.
The camels stretched their necks and legs and headed across the desert.

When evening came the caravan had reached
the safety of the last oasis.

The traders decided to winter there and continue home in the spring. In gratitude, they gave Chuan and the artist their freedom. The two carved many wooden fish and heated loadstone to make magnets. Travelers were eager to buy south-pointing fish. The artist saved every coin they earned for their journey home to the warlord's palace.

You may have guessed that Chuan's fish was an early form of compass. People in China learned about magnetism in nature thousands of years ago. By the third century B.C., Chinese scientists had invented a south-pointing compass made with a magnetic spoon that spun on a board. Records have been found of compasses in medieval China shaped like fish and turtles.

You can make your own fish compass:

- Draw a fish on a Styrofoam cup and cut it out.
- Rub a paper clip across one pole of a magnet thirty or forty times, in one direction only.
- Slide the paper clip onto the fish.
- Float the fish in a bowl of water. It will align itself north-south.